The Golden Goose Hour

The First *Shore Poets* Anthology

Edited by

Brian Johnstone

and

Rosalind Brackenbury

TARANIS
B o o k s

Design by Alan Mason   6/12/95
Printed by Clydeside Press, 37 High Street, Glasgow.

ISBN 1 873899 80 7

The publishers are grateful to The Scottish Arts Council for their financial assistance in the publication of this volume. The publishers acknowledge an award from the Deric Bolton Poetry Trust towards the publication of this volume.

Acknowledgements are due to the editors of the following magazines and anthologies in which a number of poems contained in this publication have previously appeared: Northlight for "At Barra Airport" & Pomegranate (Stramullion) for "At the Window" - Elizabeth Burns; The Scottish Child for "The Common Porpoise" & Poetry Ireland for "Beyond the Ninth Wave" - Gordon Meade; The New Edinburgh Review for "Ephemera" & The Steeple for "The Ritual Bath" - Deborah Moffat; Grafitti for "Deep Water Terminal" & The Salmon for "Water Man" - Morelle Smith; Northern Exposure (Arrival Press) for "Shetland Times" - Brian Johnstone.
Acknowledgements and thanks also to Polygon for permission to use "Stretch Marks" and "Reviewed" first published in *Coming Out With It* (1992) by Angela McSeveny and to Bloodaxe for permission to use "The Republic of Fife" first published in *The Queen of Sheba* (1994) by Kathleen Jamie.

The Editors would also like to thank the following musicians who performed during the first year of *Shore Poets* events, contributing considerably to their success; Hugh Dailly, Jan Wightman, John Young, Jan Swanson, Sandy Semeonoff, Ann Ward, Peter Thomas, Norman Chalmers & Rebecca Knorr.

SHORE POETS

In the summer of 1991, Brian Johnstone and Rosalind Brackenbury met at The Shore Gallery in Leith where they talked about the lack of regular opportunities for poets to read their verse and try out new or unfinished work on an audience. With the backing of John Young, who was running The Shore Gallery, they initiated monthly gatherings of poets and musicians. Adopting the name *Shore Poets*, they succeeded in attracting an enthusiastic and growing audience to a venue where the work of Scottish artists was also on view.

Despite the subsequent closure of The Shore Gallery, the group carried on. The first move, thanks to the encouragement of director Andrew Brown, was to the 369 Gallery in the centre of Edinburgh, where the monthly audience continued to grow. *Shore Poets* now have as their regular venue The Ceilidh House at the Tron Tavern, Hunter Square. There, under the auspices of manager Alan Cameron and supported by the Scottish Arts Council, the group has expanded and audiences further increased. Through their regular monthly events, and appearances outside their home base, they continue to play a vibrant part in Scotland's literary life.

Since its inception, the group members have seen their principal purpose as providing a platform for less published poets to read alongside the more established names from Scotland and beyond. This anthology, containing contributions from all who read during the first year of the group's activities, is ample evidence that *Shore Poets* are living up to this intention.

Contents

Trois Nuits a Edimbourg

At 20,000ft the plane is motionless.
A runway rises up to meet its wheels.

First stop on our itinerary
the castle, and a gun from Mons
the main attraction
of this battlement.
From here we see more clearly,
we photograph ourselves.

I look up, out across the firth.
What language do they speak in Fife?

We're at the edge ,
on the fringes of the Celtic fringe;
bere bannocks, usquebaugh,
salt-herring cooked
over a small peat fire.

From Waverley a voice
is misheard on the wind,
"The 10.15 to Giverny
has been delayed."

In Monet's garden
the waterlilies are preserved
in paint and water
and, like a map of France
with boundaries blurred
and coastlines indistinct,
shrunk onto postcards.

In the Grassmarket
I drink cafe au lait,
sit beneath a parasol
that advertises German bier,
watch from shelter
rain and beggars on the street.

"Cinq francs, monsieur?"

J'écris une carte postale.
Here are the headlines;
no running with Pamplona's bulls,
no pieces of the Berlin wall for sale.
Sans frontieres, c'est ordinaire

"Wish you were here."

Duddingston Loch at Dusk

Stale bread we brought for swans and urchin coots
instead is hijacked by beerbellied geese.
Already overfed their crops bulge huge
as jostling mobwinged round our poly bag
they scream a hunger that has no relief.

A distant heron, standing off amid
the silent reeds, is more fastidious
and feeds with a patrician attitude.
Or else might herons be more numerous?

Close in, the water's thick like a putrid soup.
Here dead things float, ducks strain for crumbs and swans
self-consciously parade their elegance.

The air's awhirr with insects when, ever
at the edge of sight, a batwing flicker
betrays the night that is carnivorous.

Back to the car. "Make sure you wipe your feet."

In Essaouira

We always knew there'd be a place
where North Atlantic winds converge
on Africa as we went down
for sardines and cigarettes among the nets
with Mr James and his lieutenants,
and after work there would be time
for mint tea and talk in the Place Moulay Hassan.
Women in haik sat like pillars of salt
and hooded men strolled hand in hand
by children rapt on the mosaics...

We knew dusk must adjust its shawl
by the Red Cafe, round the hammam,
and desert winds disturb those birds
hung in their cages in the hall.
Soon all we've said and done will be
blown over the ocean without farewell -
the residue glitters as salt on the tiles,
or in eyes with the sheen of windows facing the sea.

In The High Atlas

"Dust on our bags and our capes."
Nose clogged, throat choked,
couldn't speak fair to any man
"All bloody buggers round this place."

Once, under midday sun
a golden wheel
whirred by without stopping.

Days without shade,
nights without stars,
even our mule avoided us.

They say poets sing.
There's a lotta loose talk.
Guess I came near to croaking.

*

        Dawn - cold - we stumbled through
a fault in the badlands, scunnered,
dumfounert, disjaskit, boots shot,

lips split, our stubborn mule
the only optimist left
as we clattered down that gulch.

But halfway down, the badlands shrugged
or the mule kinda changed it's mind
the way history does once in a while:

> A slash across the hillside opposite
> glittered like a blade -
> below it everything bled Green.

The mule shucked its baggage and ran.

*

Up front she sang
"These Boots Are Made For Walking".
Following, my companion hummed
"Halfway To Paradise" -

She turned and looked at him
and between them flew something
like a pass, so quick I couldn't tell
who now held the ball,
but something had been exchanged
and happiness was punted into the sky
where it hung for hours, descending only
at dusk when we entered the village -

She caught and wrapped it in her arms
for tomorrow, for the badlands.

At Barra Airport

We've wandered all morning on the runway
dabbling in sea water for shells
looking out to Eriskay
and the blue Uists

Reaching the airport, we go in for coffee
windswept, sand on our shoes
The phone rings but no one answers it
All the chairs are turned towards the view

Out again, with the ocean
humming in our ears
we sit down to picnic on the dunes
and up snuggles the airport cat

People begin to gather: porters
the post bus, an ambulance
a man wih cameras
Everyone eyes the horizon

And here it comes now out of the clouds
dipping over water, skimming with white wings
Fragile as a dragonfly
it lands, on tiptoe, on the cocklestrand

A bustle of luggage and hugging
News arriving: letters and papers
Trucks scrawling tyremarks on the sand
The cat hissing at a sheepdog

The air hostess struggles with high heels
and the wind flapping at her kilt
The pilot stops for a moment bends down,
picks up a shell

At the Window
(from a painting by Chagall)

See the golden crescent of the moon
a lantern in the twilight blue
and beyond, the shadow of another
darker, bluer, midnight moon

See in the lantern moon glow
a fir tree brushed with frost

See the snow-cloud white as washing
drifting over green fields
where it's already spring
and the trees are frothy with blossom
and the farmers rest in the sun

See on the green walls of the room
a faint white strippling of flowers
like lily-of-the-valley

And see him hovering above
a figure of a man with wings
reaching out to pluck the bunches
of painted lily-flowers

See a woman in a warm red blouse
rising from her wicker chair
to stroke the cat that crouches
on the sill, about to jump
into the frosty, woodsmoke night
into the green fields, into the snow

See the angel-man bend down and touch
with fingertips as soft as snowfall
the curved red shoulder of the woman

See her smiling as she breathes a waft
of lily-perfume, as she climbs
onto the black-furred back of the cat

See them leap together from the window
into the green fields, into the snow
into the blue sky, into the cloud

See the sprinkling of frost
the scattering of blossom

See them flying through winter and spring
see them flying up into the space
that deep blue place
between two moons

Knoydart

Space enough and more for anyone who needs it;
acres of bog and heather, more liquid than land,
perforate each tract of hill and hill and then some.

Seven hours it took us, stumbling full-packed,
skirting lochans till we came on Sourlies
jauntily perched on the water's edge,
cocking a snoot at a wild Atlantic's finger-hold.

        To think that people lived here.

Settled in the mirk of a capital pub,
a grey day's paper-shuffling done,
my brain begins to reel once more
around that day on Luinne Bheinn -

        an eagle frozen in its perfect sky

        the deer we startled from its dream

        and a pale moon rising over Sgurr na Ciche,
           brittle-cold and big as a factor's fist.

Tonight, the North Wind

Tonight, the north wind brings driving rain,
Causing certain fears to grow -
The roof we had repaired last winter,
The cats who have not been seen since tea-time;
Our children who are asleep upstairs.

I think of that day in summer, after the storm,
Walking back from Stob Ban along Coire a'Mhusgain
Where we almost crossed a stream by a stone
That wasn't there; a white fleecy stone, drowned lamb
Washed down in the spate off the hills.

I would have left it there, nature taking her course
Undisturbed, but you reached in and fished it out,
Thinking of other walkers who might stop to drink.
"Not long dead," you said, holding it by a stiffened leg
Before you laid it gently on the heather.

We'd gone barely twenty yards when the ewe emerged
From behind the rock and tentatively made her way
Towards the carcass, nudged it with her snout
Once, twice, before looking back at us, dumb-eyed,
As if somehow we could explain her loss.

The cat flap creaks but only the wind comes in.

Later, we go upstairs and stand for ages in the dark,
Listening hard to the sound of our children breathing.

The Golden Goose Hour

It is the golden goose hour,
October's sun sunk
in first frost, evening
gulldrift, long sporadic snow,
settles ripple thick.

Rookfall, black film played backwards
as they rise again
overamplified as usual.
Then the geese begin.

Gossiping gaggles, skeins and skeins,
unlinking chains, and one lone
isolationist bugling home
calling his own tune
softly to himself.

Ducks quarrel while squirrels downcast
beechmast, robin throbs
with fluency. Wind slackens
while mountain blackens. Finally

the golden goose hour's curfew's
tolled by bats.

Landseerscapes

Smouldery October catches
in the mountain's thrapple,
corries belch a song of stags
 - lusty cadenzas in the hags

where black broths of peat
embalm the wallowing flanks
of rancid roques, royals, and all
the rut's also-rans. Wall-to-wall

gabbro-to-gabbro echoes
of stag-to-stag challenge
rebound, rebound, among
the coy curved heads of hinds. Flung

winds stir the cauldron's brew
to steamy fermentations
of Landseerscapes, but brushed with fire
 - autumn's flamed attire's

a garb Victorians
dared not wear, too gay,
un-gray, undismally intruding on
propriety's palette. Now sun

ignites a hill of pungent autumn dreams:
it is not all it seems.

Other peat-black ruts
imprint their lusts
upon the hill (they also roar)
 - the scarry spoor of 4x4

sheik-encrusted convoys
climb with quadrophonic
air-conditioned ease to play
privilege's games, to slay

this stag or that without
so much as breaking sweat
or chilling to the bone.
And how could they have known

that fourteen generations of MacKays
(the ghillie's tribe) were swept
from here to Canada for sheep
then deer, then accents rooted deep

in Sussex or Saudi? And how
were they to know the ghillie's gaze
blackly bore them courteous hate
for blood that flowed in spate

a human Gulf Stream rampant in reverse?
They jargonised his birthright
in The Scotsman and The Field
- "sporting estate" - a bargain sealed

in whispered millions over lunch
his week's wage couldn't buy
and played with their lifelike Landseer
three weeks a year.

from
Hominaje a la Natividad

VISIONS O OSIAN

that will nae mair like MACRIMMON return
nor come doun the faerie glen
the tale to re-tell on the straund:

birks o siller, gouden gorse,
rowans rid as onie rose,
the vera rocks an streams rehearse,

"OSIAN nae mair!"

nor will nae mair wi eagle e'e
oure-luik the muir fae the eyrie
nor gie the fowre wins the hale story:

the lav'rock we pyne sa sweet,
the plaintive bittern in the reed,
the peesers, as they tumble, greit,

"OSIAN nae mair!"

nor will he, whan the day is dune
stacher doun by auld COQ FAIRM
nor roun-about the ingle sing:

nae clarsach welcums peep-o-day,
nae bard in buskin sclimms the brae,
our man's wi the faeries, faur away:

empty hovels, ruifless haas,
roustit amang daurk, mould'rin waas,
lament, in skirls, the verra craws,

"OSIAN nae mair!"

an yet upo the drover's road
gaes oure the muir, I thocht I heard,
or seemed to hear, out-oure the yird,

       this antrin, rare
       sweet, sad note
       that telt, for sure

that OSIAN wis thare!

loups the gay beck
the freshet daunces
lambs' tails whiten the burn,

bobbed in the slack
licht aery flounces
o milkwort, bracken an fern,

giddily spin as the watter advaunces
oure boulders rolled doun fae the cairn,

in the freath-quaet pools
a river god tolls
the hours as they pass
on seven faem-bells:

watter slaps babble
a rain-swoln 'alt'
murnes for the place whaur she rose,

blae-berries dabble
thir tongues in the pelt
o the peat-tawny rill as he faas,

plumb doun the gulley
but oh, he has dwelt
wi the faeries, an he hauds by weird laws,

he lauchs at the fates that ha doomed him
                                        nae dool,

kicks up his broun houves
an syn, loups fae the pool.

ACHILLES wilna come out his tent!

has yon quyne been taen fae him?
the ane he chose, fae aa the lave
sa bonny?
                        AGAMEMNON
pitts in his claim, says
                        "hey timei"

o the heighest sort is due him,
                        him the king

he's up the hecht, taen the lassie wi him

ACHILLES wilna come out his tent!

the auld order is deein,
but man the result?

twa score an fowre buiks so mayhem!

Garden in November

There were the autumn trees
On the one hand, last leaves
Blowing skyward; at our feet
Unexpectedly, gentians, hardly belonging
To a Scots November.
The other world
Gathered itself under the trees,
Leading me inward, world through a mind's eye.
But there, on the other hand,
I had you, beside me.
Part of the garden? No,
But part of my being there, certainly,
Holding me to it, earthing me down.

There was the garden on the one hand,
And you, the man. Between us
We made a triangle. Perspective changed
In your prescence.
A matter of gender, was it?
A malting whole?
You seemed small and contained
Under the wind-tossed trees,
But necessary for a woman in Eden,
Trying to recapture dimension.

Out To Tea

"I'm not keen on cut flowers," she tells me,
"I don't like to think of them dying slowly
For my entertainment.
A friend brought them.
What was it you were asking?"

I had not yet asked,
Though questions burned, unrelieved:
Your first poems, published before you were twenty,
And your two husbands, both buried long ago,
And the love affair, blazoned in certain papers
In the thirties, those articles you wrote
On women's rights.
And the books - I look around her room
But do not see them anywhere -
"Your books..."

"Do you mind if we go in the kitchen?
I have to make the tea myself.
Will you have China? The tea caddy
Was sent home by my brother, from Canton
Before the War. There is Indian, if you prefer,
In the coronation tin."
She fumbles, as if the place were not familiar.
The kitchen is cold and empty,
It's shelves arranged by someone else
Who has left a teapot with two cups on the trolley,
And cupcakes in a tin.

We put cakes and biscuits on the plate prepared for them,
Pour milk into a gold-rimmed jug.
"I have been reading your novels," I say,
"In the new edition, with the introductions by..."
"And a little milk goes in that saucer."
She commands, but does not bother to explain.
I follow her, pushing the trolley carefully
Into the drawing room where a grey cat waits.

"His name is Whistler,
I forget why. We have no spaniels now.
Could you put the saucer on the hearth
By the fire dogs. Yes"

"In the thirties, your political involvement -
Your speeches on the rise of fascism..."
"I had short hair too, but not as short as yours.
It was considered radical; I admire it.
I love to see the bone structure, the
Strong curves of women's heads."

Silenced, I blush, from my collarless shirt
To my cropped hair: I had forgotten blushing.
I stare at my scuffed boots, swallow
Half a cupcake whole.
I can't take notes; my hands are full of cup and plate
And unaccustomed saucer.

Withered hands, heavy with rings
Placed on her fingers to commemorate
The unimaginable past, what have you touched?
Do you still remember how it felt?

I wanted to make you a lioness.
She strokes the cat, smiles vaguely.
Dust motes shine in a burst of sun
Between us. But I found you safer
Neatly contained in the green covers
Of the paperbacks that told me what you are.
Let me go now.

I am too young to know
What it is one thinks
When all the rest is over.

"This book which I have just been given
Was reviewed last week in *The Observer*.
War is unbearable, but you know that.
I was writing a sonnet about it
Just before you came in."

Notes on American Power
(with acknowledgements to J.G. Ballard)

I first heard of the 7th fleet in 1954, soon after McArthur nearly "nuked"
Korea.
But then America to me was my friend Butch who played baseball
And the lady my parents knew with the pearl handled pistol in her handbag
Who worked for the C.I.A. Butch and I chewed gum and played war games
In the rusting sand filled wrecks of tanks along the beach
And once a year got good seats to watch the Generalissimo's American made
army
Parade deafeningly through Taipei. While cooks and houseboys were called up
To crouch under shell fire on the honeycombed rocks at Quemoy and Matsu
We sang "Back to the Mainland" with the amah
But never got back there, to the land that didn't (officially) exist.

America was status filled as the air conditioning at the "Friends of China" club
Where we went ten pin bowling and the ragged Chinese boys replaced
The pins we rumbled over; as the school with clean iced water
And paper cups where cycle rickshaws waited in the noonheat to carry us
home.
I can taste even now the "C" rations at Sun Moon Lake, the steaks we ate,
The sweetened condensed milk of your bounty, America.
Every Christmas I hoped for the U.S.S. Saratoga from the P.X.*
Where all nations schemed to shop, and carefully stuck
Your airforce emblems onto the Mustangs and Tornadoes that I made.
In my 3D pop up books your skyscrapers
sprang from the page like missiles ready for the launch...
...Never did I think of you as other than generous and good,
While the eyes of an old cruel continent gazed obsequiously on
An ignorant child noisily firing his plastic Colt .45
Who returned to England with an accent that took years to lose.

* The American shopping compound where the best quality goods were sold and for which a permit was
required that was extremely valuable.

The Backward Spring
(for Jonathan; b. 13/9/85 d. 8/11/85)

Cold wind shrinks rain puddles.
Stars glint beyond a watery unstable sky;
Day breaks; the season roots
And reaches through the earth
Busy about so many births.
Buds push to blossom, though some lie
Buffeted from trees before they bloom,
Close curled and cool in thickening grass.

His absence alters all the uses of this room,
Where untouched toys lie silent and entranced
Awaiting curious hands to lift the spell. I dress here now,
And as an amputee can sense
The limb still there although it's gone,
So twinges of awoken love distress this dullness

And subside to bleak certainty.
There is to be no natural pride,
No rich language of reminiscence.
Just a small ghost pedalling air,
Stomach distended with milk
Whose folds of flesh were fattening,
Whose vanishing has cancelled all our care.

The Common Porpoise

On a stretch of sand
In north-east England, I found
A common porpoise wedged

Between two rocks,
The sprinter of the ocean's waves
Disqualified, his running

Stopped. Deep welts
Of red upon his back, and half his
Grinning face ripped off.

He'd died at sea,
The victim of a blind propeller's
Sweep. And that was how

I found him, my first
Encounter with the cousin of the dolphin.
Not leaping through Marineworld's

Circus hoop, not ploughing
Through a furrowed wave, but leaping
Far too far for me to reach,

Plunging headfirst
Into the runnels of a sandy beach.
I knew him not as a well-

Honed athlete of the sea,
But only as a walker of the land,
Like me. His victor's wreath

Not made from the leaves
Of the sweet bay laurel, but from
The row of broken shells

Found crushed beside
His gaping mouth, his row on row
Of spade-shaped teeth.

Beyond the Ninth Wave

What are you given
To start with? A boat -

No oars, no sails, no rudder,
A knife, a flask of water.

Beyond the ninth wave
This is all you need.

Oars are useless.
Your strength soon wanes.

Sails are useless.
There is no wind.

A rudder is useless.
The horizon shows no land.

The water is useful.
All around you is salt,

And the knife is useful
To cut out useless thought.

Frae Atween thi Crummlin Gables

Come ben   come away ben
staun atween ma crummlin gables
ma aegin shooders
gie oot nae notion o heat
bit beild yae frae thi granite winds

Come oan ben   come away ben
even though ma innermaist sowl
wuz scattered wae thi ashes
o thaut last open fire
whin thi Laird browt back thi herds o sheep
tae gnaw thi hert fre hill ind glen

Come ben   come oan ben
tae ma empty shell
in silence ah gie yae ma pocket o thowt

Yae hear me in thi mercilous gales
crashin through thi daithmen conifers
yae hear me fa'in through the undergrowth
as heavy drops o rain
oan silent morns.

Our Bowl of Fruit

Night after night we spend
watching our bowl of fruit
that sits upon the coffee table
what a colour the oranges are
and the bananas a beautiful banana yellow
the arrangement is something else
nothing phallic or x rated
just good clean fruit arrangement
good enough to wean the children on
the colour does go in time
the oranges lose their sheen
the bananas their brightness
but it's cheap entertainment
so we're only too happy
to replenish our bowl
whenever needs must
we have tried synthetic fruit
when the real is out of season
but the seams of dull plastic
are there for all to see
at times we pay that little bit more
but you just can't beat
a good bowl of fruit.

Island Retrospective
(In memory of Ben Franklin, sculptor, d. Nov. 1986)

Reaching a stone from the shelf, you cupped its lustre
          into a pool of water,
rubbing the granite depths with large rough
          thumbs that worked like surf.
What you said was burnished, stayed engrained
          Turned in the sea's hand

As your dust now is turned in earth. I muster
          out of the air's stir
words to carve, as you from harder stuff
          freed space for grief or love -
limbs stirring, leaves that stone imprisoned,
          your chisel tapped and found.

Yet you stayed locked, an island on whose rough shore
          friendship at times would fracture.
Eyes flashing, beard thrust out like a cliff,
          you were stony with hurt, reproof.
Island weather, clearing - as when you summoned
          all of us to your pond

where a dragonfly worked free of nymphal armour.
          Wet wings dried to a shimmer
in the space of one carved hour. I still have
          the dry, split slough
of that kingfisher insect, the monstrous husk jettisoned
          as it climbed on the wind.

Colonsay's island silence lies heavy on pasture
          and shore. It compels the ear
to unravel larksong, harsh cries of ravens far-off,
          bees grazing the turf.
And round us, like a quern, the stone-horizoned
          sea, its patient hand.

Rough Translations

Siberian air, uprisings from the Arctic
Heaving subversive volumes, ran you aground
In Fife; and though you rose as the tide turned,
And vanished, you stuck as two words in cyrillic
Holding a cargo of green and murmurous language.
Your Russian sibilants sang, like forest trees
Before the chain-saw's bitter cadences,
Znamya Oktobrya - a flag like a soiled bandage
Bleeding upon the air as on your streets,
Soaked in meaning, wrung out like a dream.
On Kinkell Ness, the sea translated from memory,
Breaking in pages, and our hands ached in our pockets
And did not wave at your Russians with unknown names
Who seemed too ordinary for their history.

The Russian trawler, *October Flag*, ran aground in heavy seas off St. Andrews in February 1987

Stretch Marks

My growing pains weren't physical.
I didn't feel the push and pull
of my lengthening skeleton.

but the white lines show
where my skin took the strain

and the mole on my breast
once lay flat against my ribs.

Reviewed

I'm hot with embarrassment
reading this considered paragraph.

Inevitable it has loomed at me
ringed in my mind like obligatory
gym periods at high school.

It's the first time since PE
that I've been called
just my surname:

four grim syllables hurled the length of the pitch
where I floundered in mud,
face like a flushed turnip.

I'm exposed like my legs
as they mottled blue and red
on the hockey field.

A moment drenched in shame
as if I'd missed a catch,
fallen flat.

In the distance Mrs Turner bawls
"McSeveney, run it under a cold tap!"

Leavin

Ah wanted ye tae leave that nicht
An yet yer leaven raxed ma hert.
Yer quiet gaun in wi sic a different pert.
Nae birse tae mak the dede mair richt.

The room is quiet noo yer gaun,
Jist the cauld reek fae the fire that's oot.
Yer warmth upon the tuim chair like a doot.
Ah never heard the door sae sauchtly drawn.

Aince we were lovers but ah jist mind the pain.
My path is taen an withergate,
While yours maun tak ye tae a different fate
And yet tonicht, ah feel alane.

Smourich

Ae smourich in a trysted place,
Twa chiels upon a silly hurl,
Must tak us oot this state o' grace,
Tae hochmagandie's rap an swarl.

Here in the mirk ah hear oor cries
A plashin fank o limb an soond,
An nark the measure o yer sighs,
That airts me through the gallus roond.

Then frae this skink o shakkin bane,
The claucht that dinnles in its thraw
This chirt that's everything an nane
Cams this remeid that redds us aw.

Sleep now my luve the sleekit licht
Has smooled aroond oor hinmaist lust,
The black eternity o nicht
Has passed away as aw things must.

Ootside the licht sae dark an steeked,
Graws dim an grey aroond the was,
An shapes that frae the darkness keeked
Are gaithered roond like humphit craws.

Ah haud ye close, ah hae nae gash
Tae spak thochts like a gleg tongued haiver.
Baith scaured and whupped by life's cruel blash,
Time gies this blink, his orra favour.

Typography in Winter

Mark your words on me, the spread
of pristine snow
commanded urgently. We hopped
the dyke
to scrawl a wish.

Near the gate we found a different story
written bold. Four small paws
scurrying desperate yards, edge
of a wing, a talon-scratch, then nothing
but the dreadful snow.

A Night in Stoer Lighthouse

Here a hungry man
could chew up the Atlantic
and still feel need of salt.

Can you smell the sun go down?
Extend a surreptitous hand to touch
the moon's deep cavities? A fox
surrounds the lighthouse with it's bark.

Your body sprouts tattoos
of whaling ships; the eiderdown is sea-haar,
bedposts timbers decked in weeds.

I reach under green sheets
to dredge
a bucketfull of sailors, drowned
as drowned can be. A prowling moth
flaps round the lightbulb
in a breeze, traversing
through the open oceans of our dreams.

Blood atmospheres return, the walls
recalled by seagull tides of dawn. The fox
is earthed: the sun erects
it's peepshow
in a fragrant void.

The Republic of Fife

Higher than the craw-stepped
gables of our institutes - chess-clubs,
fanciers, reels & strathspeys -
the old kingdom of lum, with crowns agley.

All birds will be citizens: banners
of starlings; Jacobin crows - also:
Sonny Jim Aitken, Special P.C.
whose red face closed in polis cars

utters *terrible, ridiculous*
at his brother and sister citizens
but we're no feart, not of anyone
with a tartan nameplate screwed to his door.

Citizen also: the tall fellow I watched
lash his yurt to the leafy earth,
who lifted his chin
to my greeting, roared AYE!

as in YES! FOREVER! MYSELF!
The very woods where my friend Isabel
once saw a fairy, blue as a gas flame
dancing on trees. All this

close to the motorway
where a citizen has dangled,
maybe with a friend clutching
his/her ankles to spray

PAY NO POLL TAX on a flyover
near to Abernethy, in whose tea rooms
old Scots kings and bishops in mitres
supped wi a lang spoon. Citizens:

our spires and doocoots
institutes and tinkies' benders,
old Scots kings and dancing fairies
give strength to my house

on whose roof we can balance,
carefully stand and see
clear to the far off mountains,
cities, rigs and gardens,

Europe, Africa, the Forth and Tay bridges,
even dare let go, lift our hands
and wave to the waving citizens
of all these other countries.

The Prophetess

In photos of the prophetess you can hardly see
The flamethrower strapped to her back.

Helicopters land on her obscure island.
An old sick man recalls for the journalists,

"I breathed the prophetess's nicotine.
She healed me through passive smoking"

A crone boasts: "I drank with her. She let me sacrifice
My liver that we might have life."

It's no longer clear that the prophetess
Strictly adhered to that small ridiculous sect;

Instead she is called the contemporary
Of people she never met.

After the auctioneer has sold her shoes
Singly, and put under the hammer

The view from her toilet window,
Her face is seen on laundered banknotes

And appears on Bailiffs' teeshirts.
"I sold drugs for her; my son was her amanuensis."

The sly local priest remembers her and is frightened
By the wordplay in her Holy Books.

Ephemera

Dreams die, between Dublin and Donegal.
Hopes (harboured in a warm Bewley's Café
Against the Dublin damp and chill,
Nurtured with Irish chocolate and bitter coffee),
Expand and demand elaborate attention: details
Are laid down carefully like matchsticks;
A delicate, cautious structure
Emerges from a memory.

Dublin is cold and wet. The grey walls of Trinity
Glower down the outside traveller.
But gay city colours, red cheeks, copper hair and cobalt eyes
Resuscitate the scenery; Dublin is alive.

Dreams die, and memories lie.
We face each other warily, pale eye to pale eye,
In Nancy's pub while Nancy herself piles the turf high
On the fire and smoke blues the room.
You're singing a different tune now;
Baleful Belfast ballads have intervened
And Nancy's rings with silence as we re-introduce ourselves,
Two melting icons from frozen dreams.

Ardara at noon: Irish whiskey warms our bones
And holds our eyes entombed in the golden glass.
You've found another muse, our dreams
Diverge; your Ireland is not mine,
You've left your Ulster home behind.
Nancy finds us foriegn, and between us, as between strangers,
Understanding lies fallow, words spill forth
And die; our illusions unravel, decoded
In the sunburst stream of whiskey wisdom.

Dreams have died, and died and die again,
And memories wither on the mind's vine and fold
In among themselves, condensed. They hold intact
Images and scenes, but thoughts and meaning
Evaporate, as, blown wild along the west slope of Slieve League
On Donegal's stark Atlantic flank
We let loose our 1st dreams and watch them
Lose their way south towards Killala Bay.

The Ritual Bath

You get in,
Drained of all your blood,
Your veins stripped open,
Your flesh plucked clean,
Rock salt plugging up your wounds,
Your head shorn, severed, cast aside;
Thus we prepare for sacrifice:
The slaughtered lamb,
The woman for the man,
Man before God.

One day, there is a catastrophe.
We reach the altar
Unprepared, unclean.
No one can eat.
No one dares copulate.
God turns his wrathful eye away
And leaves us howling in despair.

Now every man is his own God.
We have no need for sacrifice,
Nothing to spare.
A green slime lines
The abandoned bath;
Only a trickle of contaminated water
Leaks out over a barren land.

The Reivers

reid the fire i the reivers face
hoose flames an reed burns
bairns scream an weemin moan
men tae horse run roarin

test the flicht owre torn launds
cattle baists sweit an foam
the het trod horns bark in derk
hooves sperk in the dawin

owre the burn atween the haws
the bleck roads worth the kennin
rise oan heather gaitherin licht
watch their wecht their pechin

tak the shy road atween the rides
slow them noo in skylark quiet
slyly mak the hameward wie
steel i the ashet a tale for tellin

twae times noo the fued is focht
i the burnin an the killin
hide the baists three days are up
noo tae toast the cunnin

steek the vetts fire the fire
elbie the bellows sing the sang
wine the shade o the brithers bluid
deid an shot i the dawin

three sisters brithers lost anaw
oan the border side left deein
the morn wiel gang as tak them hame
frae a raid that wiz worth the seein

noo the reivers face is reid wie fire
the lang sangs worth the tellin
the baists are safe steekt i the byre
an the kirkyaird bells are tollin

Rape

Its back again
sprawlin owre the hill
gauche in a bricht weskit
flawntin fuu yit disjaskit

Its back again
a Friday nicht brichtness
amin the darg o a Monday mornin
wheezin oot its kisty warnin

Its back again
no quite a neep
mair a floorin simmer kind
a brasica wie a cuckoos mind

Its back again
pushin oot the oats
frae an auld kitchen table
thats sooked up mair than its able

Its back again
restrictit oure the watter
it gets free reign in these airts
unfettert touch tae awe pairts

Its back again
surroondin schails
bairns breathin like miners
in this a kintra athoot minders.

Dead Poet's Doing

So there
you were
stuck in the middle
of Sunday breakfast
your own home
company female
and singular

Have you ever been reading
in public she asked
the things (female) people ask
and had to

plärren
was the word she used [panic stations]
no average cry weep sob
but loud
uncontrolled
no concessions to etiquette
what folk fink

you thought about confessing
belly-laughs instead [safety first]
-- while in a city-centre restaurant for instance
on a Saturday night
eating alone - AND READING [you posed; bravado]

and /or about reading
on a Glasgow train
as a deliberate [settling down now]
provocative

political
action
aye look: a book
and it's a gut laugh
by the way

it's easier to admit to laughter
than to male tears
you know fine well
yet you found yourself
going ahead anyway but straight up
and telling her about Carver
Raymond   he died the summer before last
aged fifty American
and the other day
you'd been confined to bed
and read
A NEW PATH TO THE WATERFALL
his last book
in an hour
and a half

she spoke your name
made it sound like reproach
two syllables worth
well I was sick you protested
and anyway no one saw me

then by way of quick explanation
you mentioned Carver's alcoholism
& near-death &
the unexpected
ten years' grace
& remarkable out-put

and knowing
fine
he would die
first
he wrote a poem
anticipating the death
of his poet
wife
to express
to *Tess. Tess. Tess. Tess*
how he would have
grieved her

but it wasn't that poem
that got to you

another imagines
his own death
instructions
how to
respond
as he dies

brief
precise
last-minute
commands
requests
all imperative
and finally executed
you knew from the widow's introduction
each followed by words to comfort

reassuring
that's right
he her
the dying the surviving
quiet calming

one minute kiss me hard
and the next let me go
insisting as he had to
in love
in death
that's it
remember

and you who only had to
red about
that August night
couldni cope wi this [nor could she, shit, you could
                              see it in her eyes]
soon sensed
you'd have to give in
let grief be
let grief go

there's full stops everywhere but [you continued
                                    regardless]
they carve you up
stem the flow
per short line several
periods for - what?
and he's getting shaky
wobbly but controlled
(by him) responses

from you
they well, shift
you try not to splash

the tension starts
to get the better
and two thirds of the way
through the dozen or so lines
you just want to *plärren*   [a laugh you realise]
you force yourself but
to read on
he managed to write it didn't he
though you're not sure
you're going to get through this

you stopped
her eyes were filling with water
like up the outside
of the bath
such floods
making so little
noise none at all
you noticed and said sorry
bloody Brit apologising when
no need
all you could do

was say
what am I doing
telling you this
while she insisted
don't mind me

Deep-Water Terminal

You like names like that, you said,
The day we went to the James river,
Drove along the Old Gun Road,
Sun hot and heavy,
Trees coloured like a child's paint-box.
I stepped in the mud
And it oozed between my toes,
So I waded in the river, to clean them.
Big steamers come miles up the river, you said,
As far as deep-water terminal.

We went to Babe's restuarant before I left,
To drink some wine.
The waitress hugged two men at the next table,
She almost skipped across the floor,
Her eyes were blue and bright.
She put candles on all the tables.
It was getting dark and we were talking
About dreams, supernatural things,
And inexplicable connections between people.
You said you didn't believe in "all that" anyway,
And your face was jumping in light and shadow.

You look to the side of people, when you talk,
You rarely catch their eyes.
Hidden by so many jokes and stories,
I imagine voyages in all your dreams
Circling within the limits of your laughter.
I never dared to step within your boundaries
Although I thought I heard you calling
As if you thought that I was far away.

Water Man

He moves, intimate within boundaries,
Bounded by water.
He is intimate; he is contained.
He reaches out; he is warm.
He moves within water; bounded by water skin.
Reaches out; draws back.
I would need to scoop you up
And remember how it felt,
The rain of you.

City in rain morning.
A stair, opened door,
And someone still sleeping.
I try to figure out the gentlest way
of uncurling dreaming body.
The water man's receding back
Says its up to me.
He let me in with no hesitation
And I dither at the bedroom door.

He opens doors, the water man, leaves room,
As water always does,
But does not make decisions, only moves,
And you move with him,
Or stumble in wake.

To keep my footing, I knock on the door
And go in.
Little light from misty streets.
He wakes without change.
The air pours around him.
I am touching his fingers
To anchor the air.

To the kitchen, to make us some tea.
The water man moves and recedes
And advances and washes the air
Into one again.
At one point only can he be touched,
And at that point,
He is touched everywhere.

A Very Straight Line

In the parlour of the pub
the squirrel looped the same loop,
the morse of its belly
spelling out a monotonous distress,
front paws flip,
back paws down,
then blink,
at the same vista,
the blurred threat of a falcon
stuffed and poised,
the tatty drapes,
the light through brown bottled glass.

One day,
and I swear it was to spring me, not him,
I unhooked the cage.
He paused
spun backwards,
and sped out the door
in one straight line,
and when he should have sensed the wheels
he didn't swerve
as if this trajectory
was what he'd dreamed of,
all our circular days.

Funeral

2.30
The Minister empties his face
the better to extol.
Industriousness. Faith. Service,
each virtue dragged back
to that tired old roll of circus names.
"God has a place for the righteous", he says,
but no time it seems for awkward questions,
like where and why and how righteous,
or why it's thought he hears
those who bleat the best.
That old bugger in the box
left an uneven wake like everybody else;
there's a decent epitaph,
but no -
"We are in desperate need of God"
he is crying,
as if the converse was not exactly true.

Can Miquelet

You can forget for an hour
in the white hammock
hooked up like the old moon in the orchard

that hollyhock thin with life
and holy as a rose window,
the wind that moves it
lives also in the spaces of the heart;

evening places darkness
in the forked pits of almond trees
and light upon the leaves
upon the seas

of the almond and olive orchards
of Mallorca; light changing
and the brazen sun still up
above the hooded mountain.

Then you have to say it
in the hour of remembering
of feeling the way back,
the ancient slow dream of Europe.

Touch the old stones
make pacts of stone with flesh
and between the eye, the leaf,
the valley closing for night,

climb down from the old moon
hammocked above dusk and earth
that cradled you so long
a Mediterranean baby -

wrap the long shadow like a shawl.
Remember.

Waiting for the Music of the Spheres

When you come to the country of wind and stars
you reach it through black roads
winding beneath darkness.

when you come to the house of silence
you recognise it by the bloom on the wall
and the embroidered stair.

Barefoot on white tiles
and in courtyards filled with night
you drink the stars, await their music.

The sound of them is beyond the sound
of crickets, the dry leaf
and the voice of thunder

above the encircling sea, out and up
further than you can imagine
where dark fingers point into eternity.

One day in this lifetime of miracles
you may hear
from everything in the universe:

start now with the smallest,
the first rain
rustle upon the air

and listen, long enough
to create silences,
heart beat, pulse tick -

the soft wind rises between carobs
and in in among petals of bougainvillaea
that pleat like flesh,

wind chimes sing out
all over the island of forgetfulness
reminding again

of the spacious nights,
the coming of star song.

Shetland Times

Why do I crave this land?
Its old bones picked so bare
By the ravening wind.

Why does this land so hold
My gaze? The hills and isles
Prostrate before the storm.

Stand up! Get off your knees!
Why knuckle down to this
Mere slide, the earth's slipstream?

Whale backed, beetle browed!
Living off the fat of the land
Was never the way of it.

Le Coup d'Oeil - un film
(for Adele)

Provence. A hilltop cafe-bar. Few patrons save
a pock marked man, a woman half his age, the cat.

A car draws up. Your husband, the painter, yourself.
You take a seat. The view unfolds below the rail,

"*Trois express.*" You wait. The seats are hard.
The painter ups an eyebrow, turns his mouth aside.

"*Ne regardez pas, mais... c'est votre Durrell.*"
The message registers. Your eyes flick left.

A man not old but rounded, smoothed with age,
shares his table, fields some conversation.

Your talk continues. A hero? Not in so many words.
"*Peut-être... tu le connais?*" The head just shakes.

That negative damns an introduction. You sigh.
Each drinks some coffee. The afternoon wears on.

The cafe is an eyrie, its valley a hunting range.
Captured are yourselves, this writer, this woman.

A gambit. A sudden need to stretch, to see the view.
You slip out from your chair, move towards the rail.

Their discourse is beyond your ear. You cannot know,
you cannot steal a morsel. Durrell's eyes swing round.

A second slips between you. Eyes that met with *Clea's*
catch your look. "*Monsieur, permettez-moi...*" But no.

The writer turns. He makes to rise. You smile
but each thinks better and the moments's past

What would have been? You know what would have been.
"*Mais dites! Cet homme est peu ouvert.*" No point.

The day, the time, the summer passed. Two months.
You hear, the writer Durrell obituaried and dead,

You think of words, of thoughts not yet exchanged,
He wrote once...*better leave the rest unsaid.*

THE CONTRIBUTORS

KEN NELSON lives in Edinburgh where he works as a chemical engineer. He is active in a number of writers' groups. His collection *"Footprints on Formica"* is published by Rookbook Publications.

ANDREW GREIG was born in Bannockburn and now lives in South Queensferry. He has published a number of volumes of poetry, a novel and two accounts of Himalayan expeditions.

ELIZABETH BURNS is from Edinburgh but is, at present, living in Manchester. Her collection of poetry *"Ophelia and other poems"* is published by Polygon.

JIM GLEN comes from East Lothian and has published poetry and stories with work broadcast on Radio 4. In 1991 he was the recipient of an S.A.C. writer's bursary.

JIM CRUMLEY became a full-time writer in 1988 after 25 years in journalism. His many books, several featuring his poetry, deal with Scottish landscape and wildlife.

DANTE JACK CLEGG is ane hauf o the biordinar phenomenon *Scots Unbound*. He has focht for ten years agin the curse o a monoglot culture, screivin in Latin, Spanish and Inglis, as well as Scots.

MARGARET ELPHINSTONE teaches English Studies at Strathclyde University, lives in Edinburgh, and has two grown-up daughters. She has published three novels and a book of short stories.

MARK OGLE has written poetry since the age of twelve and believes strongly in the importance of poets reading their work aloud. Widely travelled, he now lives and works in Edinburgh.

GORDON MEADE lives in Lower Largo in Fife. He is currently Writing Fellow at Duncan of Jordanstone College of Art in Dundee and Writer in Residence for Dundee District Libraries.

JAMES P. SPENCE is from Edinburgh and was the 1991 winner of the city's *Spring Fling* competition. Writing in both Scots and English he has published two collections of poems.

ANNA CROWE lives in St Andrews where she works in a second-hand book shop and as a translator and interpreter. She was the 1993 winner of the *Peterloo Poets* Open Poetry competition.

ANGELA McSEVENY lives in Edinburgh and does various kinds of seasonal and part-time jobs. Her book of poems *"Coming Out With It"* was published by Polygon in 1992.

DOUGIE McKENZIE has recently returned to Edinburgh from South Africa. Best known as a short story writer, his poetry is written largely in urban Scots. He was 1984 winner of the Radio 4 short story competition.

IAN McDONOUGH comes from Sutherland. He now lives in Edinburgh and is employed as a rights worker in Fife. He was a prize-winner in the 1993 *Northwards* Scottish Poetry Competition.

KATHLEEN JAMIE is presently Scottish/Canadian Exchange Fellow. She has written a number of books of verse, most recently *"The Queen of Sheba"*, published by Bloodaxe and books of her travels in Pakistan and Tibet.

ROBERT CRAWFORD teaches at St Andrews University and lives in the town. He is an editor of *Verse*. He has published three collections of poems, one with W.N. Herbert, and several critical works.

DEBORAH MOFFAT was born in Vermont, U.S.A. in 1953. She now lives in Fife. Her stories and poems have appeared in a wide variety of periodicals and anthologies.

HARVEY HOLTON hails from Galashiels. Having lived in all parts of Scotland, he has now settled in the north of Fife. He is currently Writer-in-Residence for Dumfries and Galloway.

DONAL McLAUGHLIN was born in Ireland and has since lived in Glasgow, Aberdeen and Edinburgh. He teaches German at Heriot-Watt University. Both his translations and his own work have been widely published.

MORELLE SMITH is a writer living in Edinburgh. She has published two books of verse to date and her poems and short stories have appeared in various magazines and anthologies.

HUGH McMILLAN lives in Dumfries. He has twice been in receipt of S.A.C. writers' bursaries. He has brought out three volumes of poetry and been published widely both in the UK and abroad.

ROSALIND BRACKENBURY has published three books of verse, most recently *"Coming Home the Long Way Round the Mountain"*, and numerous novels. Widely travelled, she is based in both Edinburgh and Florida.

BRIAN JOHNSTONE is from Edinburgh but lives in Fife, where he teaches in a primary school. His work has appeared in many periodicals and anthologies. He is also a photographer with two solo exhibitions to date.